EMOTIONAL
HEALING
IN 3 EASY STEPS

EMOTIONAL HEALING
IN 3 EASY STEPS

PRAYING MEDIC

INKITY
PRESS™

Inkity Press, 137 East Elliot Road, #2292, Gilbert, AZ 85234

This book and other Inkity Press titles can be found at:
InkityPress.com and **PrayingMedic.com**

Available from Amazon.com, CreateSpace.com, and other retail outlets.

For more information visit our website at **www.inkitypress.com** or email us at **admin@inkitypress.com** or **admin@prayingmedic.com**

ISBN-13: 978-0998091228 (Inkity Press)
ISBN-10: 0998091227

Printed in the U.S.A.

TABLE OF CONTENTS

NOTE

Although I work as a trained paramedic, I am not a licensed counselor or mental health professional. I cannot diagnose mental health conditions or recommend the best course of treatment for them. The advice given in this book is not intended to replace the advice of a licensed counselor or mental health professional. I do not assume liability for any harm that results from a decision to forego professional mental health treatment. I cannot guarantee that the suggestions given in this book will result in the same outcomes I, or others have experienced. I am not responsible for the outcomes that result from following the advice given in this book. There is no guarantee that the teaching in the book will lead to healing. While I believe wholeheartedly in divine healing, I also believe in and encourage you to seek standard diagnostic evaluation and treatment if it is indicated.

INTRODUCTION

WHILE DESIGNING THE COVER FOR this book, my wife encouraged me to let her create something with a light-hearted and whimsical look. I asked why she didn't want to create one with a more contemporary look, like the rest of our books. She said the cover ought to convey something about the process of emotional healing we've discovered. And unlike most methods of counseling and prayer for emotional healing, the one we use isn't heavy or serious. The steps we'll outline are a lighter and less stressful approach than anything you've probably encountered before.

This isn't a comprehensive book on emotional healing. It is however, a place to begin the process of receiving healing of the emotional trauma you've suffered in the past. Rather than write a book which covers the subject from various angles, this book is narrow in scope. It focuses on a specific type of emotional trauma—one that is most commonly found in the general population—and offers a quick method to remove it permanently. Although the approach I'm going to describe can be done quickly and easily, don't be fooled into thinking it isn't powerful. Nearly everyone I've ministered to using this approach has remarked at how powerful the results were.

This book does not address the subject of deliverance. While I acknowledge that many (perhaps most) people who suffer from emotional trauma also have some level of demonization, it's my intent to focus exclusively on emotional healing. There are many books that have been written on the subject of deliverance and I've included a lengthy chapter on that subject in my book *Divine Healing Made Simple*. I do intend to write a more comprehensive book in the future on emotional healing and deliverance. As you follow the method I'll describe, you're free to use whatever deliverance techniques you're accustomed to, though you may not need them. In many cases, the emotional healing itself can remove demons effectively.

I've read many of the books that have been written on emotional healing and I've reviewed many of the current approaches being used in Christian ministry. Included in the methods I've become familiar with are *Sozo* which was developed by Bethel Church, *Immanuel Prayer, Liebusting, Theophostic,* as well as the approaches used by Freedom Encounters and the teaching series developed by Elijah House called *Healing Trauma.*

Although all of the approaches in use today have a degree of effectiveness, most of them take several hours—and in some cases—days or weeks to complete. I needed to find a method that could effectively heal emotional trauma in a ten minute ambulance transport and none of these offer a quick method for healing.

After receiving my own emotional healing and after my wife received hers, we began comparing the elements of the different approaches in use today. There were a few common elements that nearly all the different approaches relied upon. I took the handful of steps they had in common and developed a short process based on them. I tried this new approach on one person after another and the results were shocking. Nearly everyone experienced a significant level of healing of the painful memories from their past and the emotions associated with them.

Over the last year I've used this approach on over 100 people. Some of the healing sessions were done over Skype, some were done in person and many (probably half) were done over internet chat. It didn't seem to matter whether I was with the person or not. The results were just as effective over internet chat as in person or over Skype. The method can be done by just about anyone and requires no formal training. It can be done just about anywhere and in most cases it only takes a few minutes. The great thing about this method is that after someone has been healed, they can easily be taught to use the same method to help someone else receive healing. It also works well for healing new emotional wounds that happen in our daily interactions with others.

I used this approach with one woman who had been through 20 years of counseling. She said the counseling didn't help her at all. After a 15-minute chat with her over the internet, the painful emotions from the sexual abuse she suffered as a child were gone. She couldn't believe it. She was so impressed with the results she immediately used what I had taught her to get her husband healed of his emotional trauma.

I used this approach with another woman over internet chat. She said she had been through every kind of emotional healing available, multiple deliverance sessions, and years of prayer for healing of various problems. "I've repented of every sin I can think of, renounced everything under the sun and I've forgiven everyone who has ever hurt me and I still feel like hell." She was very skeptical that I had anything to offer. We used my quick approach and when we were done she was astounded. The anger and all the other painful emotions she had wrestled with for years were completely gone. She felt better than she ever remembered feeling. Then she asked how long it would last. She couldn't believe something this simple could have a lasting effect. I got in touch with her several weeks later and she was still feeling just as good as the day she was healed.

CHAPTER ONE

EMOTIONAL HEALING DYNAMICS

OUR SOUL IS SHAPED EVERY day by the interactions we have with each other. Every video we watch, all the interactions we have with our family and coworkers, and every encounter we have with God has an impact on the person we are becoming. I'm not suggesting as ancient philosophers did, that we are the sum of our experiences. However, the person we are today is largely a product of our past experiences. And if we have emotional or behavioral problems today, they are likely the result of things that happened in our past. The events of our past affect the way we feel, behave, and interact in the present. If we want to change our current behavior and emotions, we need to change the way the past has affected us. While we can't change the events of the past, we can change the way in which those events affect the way we live today.

The way in which we respond to present conflicts was shaped in our soul during our youth. When we faced one event and one challenge after another, we developed ways of responding to them. Sometimes we developed an appropriate response and sometimes not. Most of these coping behaviors are ones that we learned from our parents. If Jesus was not a part of our life when we were three years old for example, we learned to respond to such events without the light of God to guide us. And although we may have the light of God in us today, our patterns of thinking and behavior have been etched in our soul before that light was present, and it's likely that we're still responding in ways that were developed in relative darkness.

This is not to deny the reality that we are a new creation when we are born again. At the moment when the Holy Spirit takes up residence in us, we are given a brand new life. But all our wounds from the past—both physical and emotional—are not immediately healed. The healing of our body and soul is a process that takes time.

When we are young, we learn to respond to the events of life with a wide range of emotions. If we react with joy to a specific event, a memory of the event is recorded in our soul along with a record of the emotion. Later, when a similar event happens, even though we may not consciously recall the previous event, we may associate the two events and their emotions and react to the new event with joy. If we continue to react to similar events with joy, a learned response develops which tends to ensure the same response to future events that are similar.

If on the other hand, an event like being bitten by a dog causes us to react with fear, it will leave a memory and a wound in our soul associated with fear. The wound, the memory and the emotion are all connected. Events that we perceive to be similar can activate or *trigger* the wounded part of the soul. Later, when we're approached by a dog, the wounded part of the soul can be triggered along with its emotion of fear, even though the dog may be friendly.

When we experience sudden rage in the present, it's often the result of a wound in our soul related to an event from our past being triggered that causes us to feel rage. When we experience rejection, doubt, or any other negative emotion in response to an event, there is usually a wound in our soul being triggered which causes us to experience the emotion we're presently feeling.

God the Father

Because they are emotional immature, children lack the kind of Godly wisdom required to properly assign meaning to emotionally traumatic events. For a three year old, something as simple as being locked in a closet for ten minutes can be extremely traumatic. A three year old doesn't have the capacity to understand that they will eventually be let out of the closet. It's not unusual for children this young to imagine they will never get out the closet. When we revisit events from our past with the perspective we had as a child (it's generally impossible to view them otherwise) it's often difficult to see anything positive in them. But when the same events are viewed through the eyes of God the Father, we can receive His perspective and wisdom on them. His perspective imparts the wisdom we need today to properly frame the event and assign meaning to it. In the process of emotional healing, it's been my experience that the person of God the Father acts as the one who imparts the right perspective on a traumatic event. This is not a hard and fast rule, but a general guideline to use if you need a divine perspective on an event.

Jesus

The role Jesus plays in redeeming our past is generally the healer. One of the things that was prophesied about the ministry of Jesus was that He would carry away our griefs and sorrows:

> *Surely He has borne our griefs And carried our sorrows;*
> *Yet we esteemed Him stricken, Smitten by God, and*
> *afflicted. (Is. 53:4)*

This passage says that Jesus bore (carried away) our griefs and sorrows. Griefs and sorrows are painful emotions. And if He has already borne them for us, then it's not necessary for us to bear them any more. The next verse says, *"... and by His stripes we are healed."* The healing Jesus offers us is both physical and emotional. Emotional healing is a matter of allowing Him to take our painful emotions from us. The approach I use for emotional healing is to literally have people ask Jesus to take their sadness, their rejection, their anger, or any other negative emotion from them.

Jesus can also serve in different roles in the healing process. Like the Father, He's able to show us a divine perspective of a traumatic event. Many times, during a prayer session, people will see in their mind's eye a scene where Jesus is with them comforting them or crying with them during the event.

The Holy Spirit

Many people have amnesia about the traumatic events of their past. Amnesia regarding emotional trauma can be a kind of blessing. If you can't recall an event, it's hard for the enemy to remind you of it and cause you to feel shame or condemnation over it. This amnesia seems to be a protective mechanism designed by God to keep extremely painful memories from affecting the entire soul. But if you can't recall an event, it's hard to gain the Father's perspective on it. Some people have vague negative feelings that are hard to identify precisely. It's difficult to ask Jesus to take negative emotions from you, if you're unable to identify them.

Many times we experience painful emotions or exaggerated emotional responses and have no idea what causes them. In such cases, an emotional wound is being exposed, but not the past event that caused it. It's my belief that God will allow us to feel the emotion but not recall the event as a way to bring the issue to light so we'll seek healing of it. The pain we feel can drive us to seek relief with drugs, alcohol, sex and other things but that's not what God intends. His purpose is to have the wound in our soul healed and the emotion removed, permanently.

Healing of emotional pain comes when we identify traumatic events, give the emotions associated with them to Jesus and ask him to heal the wound in our soul. But if an event can't be remembered, there is a way to jar our memory. Jesus said this about the Holy Spirit:

> "I will pray to the Father and He will give you another Helper, that He may abide with you forever—the Spirit of truth… He will teach you all things, and bring to your remembrance all things that I said to you." (Jn 14:16,26)

The cure for amnesia of the events from our past is the Holy Spirit. When we visit our past with the Holy Spirit, He is able to bring to our remembrance things we've forgotten. When He uncovers traumatic events, we may feel and understand the emotions associated with them. Once the memories have been retrieved, the Father can give us His perspective on them. Jesus can take way the painful emotions and heal the wounds left in our soul by them.

CHAPTER TWO

MY EMOTIONAL HEALING

ONE DAY WHILE AT WORK, a number of small things happened that would normally not cause me much stress. As they happened I felt a little anger beginning to build. I told myself I was not going to let these things make me angry. Despite this, I spent most of the day in a very angry mood. Fortunately, I was able to sit quietly in the ambulance most of the day and my anger didn't have an opportunity to hurt anyone.

At this time, I worked with a partner who had a way of doing his job that seemed to push every button I had. I often found myself being angry over some little thing that he did. I began to wonder if perhaps God put us together to help me deal with some problem I was struggling with. I'd spent a lot of nights venting my frustration to my wife who was always sympathetic. One problem with having supportive friends is that they'll sometimes try to justify your sin. I had accepted her justification for my moments of rage, but I felt like there was something causing it that needed to be dealt with. As I reflected on past events that caused the angry outbursts, I realized they were all triggered by a similar set of circumstances.

One sign that you have an emotional wound is when you over-react to a certain type of situation repeatedly. An example is if you're usually an easy-going person that seldom gets angry. When certain situations repeatedly trigger the same type of response—in this case an overreaction of anger—there's a wound in your soul that's causing this over reaction. Some people describe it as feeling like they've temporarily become another person.

I posted about this problem on social media one day and received a message from a grateful woman who said she finally understood something about her husband that had puzzled her for years. Their family had a tradition of taking weekend vacations to the Oregon coast. Her husband was normally a very easy going man, but every time they went to the coast, he turned into a different person. She described his behavior as being almost like a bratty teenager. He was uncooperative and argumentative the whole time they were at the coast. When they returned home, his demeanor went back to normal.

This type of behavior is usually due to the triggering of memories of past experiences, which causes wounded parts of our soul to emerge and take control of our mind. Our behavior becomes like that of the person we were at the time the emotional trauma occurred.

It's been said that time heals all wounds, but the truth is that time doesn't heal emotional wounds. Rather than being healed over time, emotional trauma can plague us our entire life. Emotional trauma creates a wound in our soul much like a flying piece of metal can cause a wound to our skin. Although our skin has a way to heal the wounds it receives, our soul doesn't have the ability to heal itself.

Emotional trauma has the *potential* to affect the entire soul, but God designed a way to limit the damage of emotional trauma by allowing the soul to create what are known as *fragments*. A fragment is a part of the soul that contains the memories and emotions of a traumatic event. It's like a part of our personality that's been frozen in time. Fragments prevent the wounded parts of the soul from becoming the dominant influence over the core of the soul. In effect, the fragmenting of the soul compartmentalizes the wounds and minimizes the damage that can be done to the rest of the soul.

Fragments usually only have awareness of a single event or a string of repeated events and their related emotions. The fragment normally lies dormant in the soul until an event occurs that is reminiscent of the one that caused the fragment to be created. When one of these events happens, the fragment can be triggered and it may take control of the soul. When this happens, the person responds the way they would at the age they were when the fragment was created. If the fragment was formed as a toddler, the person may crawl on the floor or try to hide behind furniture. If the fragment was created as a teenager, the person may act like a rebellious 13-year-old. The emotions they display are not appropriate for the current situation. Instead, they are the emotions that were experienced at the time the fragment was created.

Soul fragments have as their main goal the protection of the core personality. A soul fragment will assume control when they perceive there is a threat to the individual. When a traumatized person has an experience that the fragment perceives to be a threat, the fragment takes over control of the mind, will and emotions, and the individual reacts to the situation from the wounded perspective of the fragment. The actions of a soul fragment are usually an overreaction to the situation. Soul fragments have less understanding of what is normal and acceptable behavior as compared to the core of the personality. When the threat goes away the core of the soul regains control, the fragment once again becomes dormant, and the individual functions normally again.

For example, I know a woman who has a terrible fear of going into basements. When I asked why she had this fear, she said it was because she had been molested by her uncles in a basement when she was a child. At the time she was molested, a part of her soul was wounded which created a fragment dominated by fear (and probably shame and guilt). Today, whenever she thinks about going in a basement, the fragment is triggered and she feels fear and the other emotions associated with that event.

A similar but different part of the soul that is created by trauma is known as an *alter*. Like a fragment, an alter retains the memories and emotions of specific events, but unlike fragments, alters can have unique personalities of their own that are distinctly different from the core of the personality. A person with many alters is usually diagnosed with Dissociative Identity Disorder (DID), or what was once called Multiple Personality Disorder. A severely traumatized person can have hundreds, or even thousands of alters.

When an alter is triggered by an event, the individual's will and emotions come under the control of the alter. The person behaves in correspondence to the personality of the alter, while the core of the personality is rendered ineffective. The core personality sometimes feels like an observer to what is happening to them, instead of the participant. Some describe it as like having someone drive their car while they watch from the rear seat. Sometimes the core personality is completely unaware of what's happening to them—a condition known as dissociation. When the event passes and the core assumes control again, it's not unusual for them to have no idea what they said or did during the episode.

The goal of emotional healing is to heal the fragments and alters and to reintegrate them into the soul, preventing future episodes of painful emotions and disassociation. Just prior to the day

I received my emotional healing, I had been having moments where a fragment was taking over control of my mind, and it was causing me to overreact in anger. While thinking about it and praying for understanding, I became aware that my anger was related to a series of traumatic events that happened when I was a teenager. I finally accepted the fact that I needed to be healed of the trauma.

A friend named Matt Evans, who had done a lot of emotional healing, saw my post on Facebook about my need for emotional healing. He sent me a message asking if I had time to talk the following day. We talked on the phone the next day for about two hours. During our phone conversation he took me through the process of emotional healing.

There is one general point I'd like you to consider: In order to heal the wounded soul, the part of the soul that is wounded and/or fragmented must be allowed to take over temporary control of the mind, will, and emotions. This means you will usually have to go back to an event in the past that causes the emotion to be felt strongly. In order to receive healing, the wounded soul fragment must usually meet Jesus and receive healing and instruction from Him.

The first step Matt had me take was to go back to a place in my life where I could feel the anger again. This was not hard to do. There were many places in my mind where I could go back and relive an event that would bring up the emotion of anger. Matt had me go back to one of the earliest events. When I was feeling the emotion from that event, he had me say some short prayers, which I'll list below.

One thing he requested of me was to resist the temptation to over think the situation. Emotional healing is a purely emotional issue and when you attempt to rationalize or think about what's happening it distracts your mind from connecting with the emotions you need to feel. Matt urged me not to think too much about what we were doing.

Here is the process Matt used:

1. I recalled an event that was troubling me and identified the strongest negative emotion I was able to feel, which happened to be anger.

2. I confessed to God that my anger was a sin. (Not every emotion is sinful. If an emotion is not sinful, this step isn't necessary.)

3. I said that I believed the blood of Jesus had taken away the penalty and consequences of my sin.

4. I asked Jesus to take away my feeling of anger.

5. We felt like Jesus wanted to give me something in return for giving Him my anger. I felt like he wanted to give me

His peace. So I asked Him to give me peace in exchange for my anger and I received His peace.

6. I asked Jesus to heal the wound in my soul.

When we were done with this process, Matt asked me to recall the event again and try to feel the emotions from it. I was very surprised when I recalled the event. I found that I could not feel the anger. I could remember the event itself, but the anger was gone.

The fact that I could no longer feel the anger from the event led me to believe I really was healed. The healing seems to be permanent as I haven't felt anger being triggered like I once did. This is not to say that I'll never again get angry. That's not what emotional healing does. It doesn't take away your ability to feel certain emotions. It just heals the wounded parts of your soul that are dominated by them.

I received a strange confirmation of my healing. When I arrived at work the next day, my partner, who had worked with me for the previous year, said he was being transferred to another unit. I couldn't help but think that God had finally accomplished in me what he wanted with this partner and it was time for me to have a new one.

CHAPTER THREE

EMOTIONAL HEALING IN THE AMBULANCE

THE DAY AFTER I RECEIVED my healing, I went on a call to an emergency department to transport a young woman for mental health treatment. We arrived early and as I waited for her to be ready for the transport, I read the transcript dictated by the social worker who interviewed her.

Her depression and suicidal thoughts began a year and a half earlier after she had her child. She suffered from postpartum depression that never went away. Since her child had been born, she had several outbursts of extreme anger. In one incident she punched holes through the wall of her apartment. In another incident she almost stabbed her husband with a knife. She had come to the hospital this time for treatment of depression and suicidal thoughts brought on by another incident with her husband where she was overcome by feelings of anger and tried to push him into traffic. I also read through her history where she said she had been molested as a teenager.

As I read her report, it became obvious that she was suffering from the same thing I had just been healed of. It seemed like she had a wounded or fragmented soul that was temporarily taking control during certain events and she was reacting with exaggerated anger. We loaded her in the ambulance and I spent the first ten minutes of the transport telling her about my own struggles with anger and how I had been healed the day before. She listened intently and I could tell that my testimony was giving her hope. As I came to the end of my testimony, I asked her a direct question: "I know you were molested as a teenager. Do you want him to die?"

"I don't want him to die a violent death. I just want him to die and go away."

"My friend got me healed and I think we can get you healed," I replied. "The first thing I did was go back to one of the events where I could feel the anger. Then he led me in a few prayers. When we were done, he had me go back again and try to feel the anger from the event, but I couldn't feel it any more. I could recall the experiences but I couldn't feel the anger. So here's my question: Would you like to be healed of your anger?"

"Yes I would," she replied as she put out her hand. I took hold of it.

"I need you to go back in your mind to an incident that creates a feeling of anger. When you can feel it, let me know."

It only took a few seconds. "Okay, I feel it."

"I'm going to have you repeat what I say." These are the prayers we said together:

"God, I confess my anger as sin."

"Jesus, I believe you died to take away my sins."

"I do not want to be controlled by anger anymore."

"Lord, I ask you to take this anger from me and give me your peace in return."

"I ask you to heal the wound in my soul caused by anger and I receive your healing."

She repeated everything I said. "Okay, now I want you to go back and try to feel the emotions from any of the events." She sat there for a moment then looked at me in shock. "Crazy, huh?" I said. "You can't feel the anger any more, can you?"

She immediately realized she was healed and her mind was already thinking about how this approach could be used for other problems.

"Do you think it would work for other emotions?"

"Like what?"

"Sadness."

"I think it will work for any emotion that you don't want. God can give you something in exchange for what you give Him. So if you give Him your sadness, He may give you His joy in return. If you give Him your feelings of rejection, He may give you His acceptance. I think this is something you can do yourself. I mean, you're going to be sitting here for a couple of days without much to do. You may want to sit quietly and talk with God and ask Him to heal you of all this stuff."

We arrived at the hospital and got her registered. Before we left, she thanked me for taking the time to help her. This was my first attempt at doing emotional healing with one of my patients and it seemed to be successful. The amazing thing is that it didn't take two hours but only ten minutes. In many cases, emotional healing isn't hard or complicated.

I realize that this may not be true for every person or for every situation. Sometimes emotional healing will take longer, depending on the severity of the emotional trauma. Even if we can't address every problem a person might have in the short time we have with them, we can show them the power God has over their problems and give them hope that they can one day live in complete freedom.

CHAPTER FOUR

EMOTIONAL HEALING SCRIPT

THE APPROACH I'VE DEVELOPED TO emotional healing is simple, but effective. It's one that I believe just about anyone can use and it doesn't require special training. It doesn't even require the person who needs healing to be with you. It's so easy and quick that a friend refers to it as the "one minute healing prayer." Below is a brief explanation of the process I use and a step-by-step guide. If you need healing, you might ask a trusted friend to help you with this exercise or you can do it yourself:

Note:

I've seen excellent success with this approach, but it may not be completely effective with every kind of mental illness and emotional trauma. Some people have complex issues that require several different approaches to be used in conjunction. I believe this approach may help some people with complex trauma, but others may require the use of a combination of methods in order to be completely healed. This approach seems to be most effective with the kind of emotional trauma seen in the average person.

Trigger Alert:

If you suffer from a condition such as PTSD, Multiple Personality Disorder (MPD), or Dissociative Identity Disorder (DID), the following exercise may trigger unpleasant emotions and may cause you to suffer an acute episode, which could be dangerous to you. If an alter is triggered who is prone to suicidal thoughts, you may feel like committing suicide. For your own safety, please have a trusted friend or counselor in the room that is willing to assist you, if you decide to do this exercise.

Receiving healing of painful emotions and memories can be a fairly straight-forward process that consists of three simple steps:

1. Identify the painful emotion associated with a particular event

    a. If the emotion is sinful, ask God to forgive you and receive his forgiveness

2. Ask Jesus to take the painful emotion from you

3. Ask Him to heal the wound in your soul caused by it

For many people, emotional healing really *can* be that simple. Emotions simply need to be felt. Once you've felt them, you no longer need to carry them around if they're painful. A more detailed description of the process is outlined below.

The main problem I've found with emotional healing is that people who are extremely rational by nature may ask a lot of "why" questions in the middle of the healing process, which causes distractions and impedes the healing process. It doesn't matter *why* something happened to you; the only thing that matters with regard to healing is *how* it affected you. If you focus on the emotions you're feeling, and identify them one-by-one and allow Jesus to heal them, it's likely that you'll be able to receive healing fairly easily.

Healing painful emotions usually requires you to go back to events in your life where you can feel an emotion that is troubling you.

1. Identify a painful emotion associated with a particular event

   a. If the emotion is sinful, ask God to forgive you and receive his forgiveness. Say that you believe His blood has taken away the penalty and consequences of your sin. If it is not sinful, go to the next step

2. Tell Him you want the emotion removed from your soul.

3. Ask Him to heal the wound in your soul caused by the emotion.

   a. Tell Him you receive His healing.

   b. If the emotion is there because you believed a lie about that situation, ask Jesus to show you the truth about it.

   c. An optional step that is to ask Him to give you something positive to replace the negative emotion that He is removing. If you ask Him to take away sadness, you might ask Him to give you joy. If you ask Him to take away anger, you might ask Him to give you peace.

When you're done with this, bring the memory of the painful event to your mind again. If the emotion was healed, you should not be able to feel that emotion any longer, but there may be a different negative emotion that you can feel. Determine what negative emotion is strongest and do the same thing with it that you did with the first emotion:

1. Identify the painful emotion

   a. If the emotion is sinful, ask God to forgive you and receive his forgiveness. Say that you believe His blood has taken away the penalty and consequences of your sin. If it is not sinful, go to the next step

2. Tell Him you want the emotion removed from your soul.

3. Ask Him to heal the wound in your soul caused by the emotion.

   a. Tell Him you receive His healing.

   b. If the emotion is there because you believed a lie about that situation, ask Jesus to show you the truth about it.

   c. An optional step that is to ask Him to give you something positive to replace the negative emotion that He is removing. If you ask Him to take away sadness, you might ask Him to give you joy. If you ask Him to take away anger, you might ask Him to give you peace.

When you're done, bring the memory of the event to your mind again. Once more, try to determine if there are any negative emotions. If there are, repeat this process until you can bring the event to your memory and you feel no negative emotions. This process can be used on any memories that are associated with negative emotions. When you no longer feel any negative emotions while recalling an event, you are healed.

If you suffer from amnesia concerning the events from your past, you can ask the Holy Spirit to bring to your memory the things you've forgotten. As He brings the events to mind, and as you feel the emotions, ask Jesus to heal them.

When I use this approach over internet chat, I simply type out the instructions in the chat window and ask the person to say them aloud. I tell them to let me know when they are done with each step then we move on to the next step.

If you'd like to be healed of all the emotional trauma you've received over your lifetime, you might consider beginning with the earliest memories you have that are troublesome to you. Use this process to receive healing of the emotions of that event, then go to the next event from your past that stirs up negative emotions when you think about it. You can go year-by-year if you'd like from early childhood to the present. You can do this at a pace that is comfortable for you. It might be best to allow time between healing sessions. It can be done over the course of several days or weeks, if needed.

If you apply this process to all the emotionally traumatic events you can think of, you will probably find a great deal of freedom afterward. I've seen a number of people also receive healing of *physical* symptoms of illness and injury after going through this process. If you need healing for a physical condition, you can use a standard approach for physical healing, which generally involves commanding the symptoms to leave and commanding the affected part of the body to be healed. After you've had your soul healed, you might consider keeping it healed. This approach also works well in the moment. It can be used to heal those minute-by-minute hurts, wounds and offenses we run into every day. Just give the painful emotion you're feeling to Jesus and ask Him to heal the wound caused by it.

Forgiveness

It isn't necessary to forgive those who have wounded you before you can receive emotional healing. Forgiving someone from the heart can be difficult when you still feel the emotional pain they've caused. But after you've been healed, you might find it easier to forgive them and perhaps even forget those unpleasant memories. If you are able to forgive them it will free you and it will free them. Jesus said to His disciples, *"If you forgive the sins of any, they are forgiven them; if you retain the sins of any, they are retained." (Jn 20:23)* When we learn to forgive others, it increases our own capacity to receive forgiveness both from men and from God. It can also help lessen the trauma we're likely to suffer in the future.

My Prayer for You

I pray that you would prosper even as your soul prospers. I pray that your heart would be healed and filled with peace. I pray that you would know the depth of God's love for you. I pray that you would know the surpassing riches and treasure He has held in reserve for us from the beginning. I pray that you would be filled with all faith, knowing the mysteries of the kingdom and that you would demonstrate His power. And I pray that in all these things God would be glorified.

THANK YOU FOR
PURCHASING THIS BOOK

For inspiring articles and an up-to-date list of my books, go to my website, **PrayingMedic.com**. There you will also find links to my Podcasts and other resources.

Divine Healing
Made Simple

Get honest answers to the difficult questions you have about healing and the supernatural:

- Why are my prayers ineffective when I ask God to heal someone?
- Many people have prayed for my healing— so why am I still not healed?
- Does God want me to learn a lesson through physical suffering and sickness?
- I was miraculously healed through prayer— why have my symptoms returned?

Get the answers to these questions... and many more.

In his down-to-earth style, Praying Medic presents a solid case that all believers have power and authority from God for healing. Miracles are happening every day through the prayers of average men and women on the street and in workplaces. With a little instruction, you too can learn how to release God's healing power. Exercises at the end of key chapters will help you develop your ability. With insight on many other topics including making disciples, deliverance, words of knowledge, and how God speaks to you through your dreams, this book celebrates what God is doing and shows you how miracles can become part of your everyday life.

This book is part of a series called **The Kingdom of God Made Simple** —
a self-study course designed to train believers to live the
life offered to them as heirs of God's kingdom.

Seeing in the Spirit
Made Simple

Is "seeing in the spirit" only for a few people—or can anyone do it?

If you want to see angels, demons and the heavenly realms, but have been told you don't have the gift of seeing in the spirit, this book is for you. For years we've been told that seeing in the spirit is a gift given to only a few special people or an anointing that must be imparted to us by a man or woman of God. In this book, Praying Medic presents biblical and physiological evidence to prove that seeing in the spirit is not reserved for only a few special people, but is possible for everyone.

With the same down-to-earth teaching style he used in **Divine Healing Made Simple** and **Hearing God's Voice Made Simple**, the author provides Bible-based teaching, dozens of testimonies, and illustrations that reveal the truth about seeing in the spirit. He includes exercises at the end of key chapters to help you improve your spiritual vision. Whether you're a seasoned seer or a newbie, you'll learn from the experiences and insights shared by the author. Not only will you develop better spiritual eyesight, but your relationship with God will grow too.

This book is part of a series called **The Kingdom of God Made Simple** — a self-study course designed to train believers to live the life offered to them as heirs of God's kingdom.

Hearing God's Voice
Made Simple

Is God Really Speaking?
Yes—and you can learn to hear Him.

Today, many are skeptical that God is speaking or that we can know with certainty we're hearing Him accurately. **Hearing God's Voice Made Simple** makes the case that God is speaking and that we can learn to hear Him. As you read this book, you may even discover that God has been speaking to you all along but you simply didn't know how to hear Him.

With the same straightforward, down-to-earth style used in the best-sellers **Divine Healing Made Simple** and **Seeing in the Spirit Made Simple**, Praying Medic teaches about the many ways in which God speaks. You'll find practical exercises at the end of key chapters to help develop your ability to sense what God is saying to you. Whether you're skilled at hearing God's voice, or more of a novice, this book will show you ways of hearing from God that you may not have considered—and you'll also learn what to do with the things God says.

This book is part of a series called **The Kingdom of God Made Simple** — a self-study course designed to train believers to live the life offered to them as heirs of God's kingdom.

Traveling in the Spirit
Made Simple

Is spiritual travel "astral projection" or is it a biblical practice used for God's purposes?

If you've been taught that traveling in the spirit is unbiblical or is only used by the New Age or the occult, this book is for you. The author examines accounts from the Bible which demonstrate that the prophets and apostles traveled in the spirit. He compares astral projection with Christian spiritual travel and proves that they are not the same thing. Far from being an occult practice, spiritual travel is actually a tool given to us by God to accomplish His divine purposes.

With the same down-to-earth teaching style used in **Seeing in the Spirit Made Simple** and **Divine Healing Made Simple**, Praying Medic provides Bible-based teaching, dozens of testimonies and illustrations that will help even the least experienced believer understand spiritual travel. Exercises are provided at the end of key chapters. Traveling in the spirit can help you in healing, deliverance and intercession, but most importantly, it will help you know God in a more personal way.

This book is part of a series called **The Kingdom of God Made Simple** — a self-study course designed to train believers to live the life offered to them as heirs of God's kingdom.

Defeating Your Adversary in the Court of Heaven

Are believers really able and allowed to appear in the court of heaven?

Many Christians are surprised when they first hear that the courts of heaven are real. Many more have been shocked at how their lives were changed after they appeared in court to face their adversary. Illnesses have vanished, legal proceedings have been halted and demonic attacks have suddenly stopped.

Isn't it time you learned how to present your case in the court of heaven?

With the same down-to-earth teaching style used in **Divine Healing Made Simple**, Praying Medic explains in layman's terms what the courts of heaven are and why we may want to appear in them. He shows why, when and how you can appear in the court of heaven and how you can obtain victory over your accuser. There's even a simple, step-by-step protocol that shows you exactly what to say, when to say it, and what not to say.

My Craziest Adventures with God Volume 1
The Spiritual Journal of a Former Atheist Paramedic

Does God speak today? Would He heal the sick or work miracles through you—even if you feel "average" or not particularly gifted?

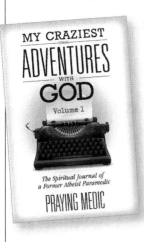

Not long ago, Praying Medic was an average guy who sat in a church pew every Sunday wondering if there was more to the Christian life than this. After losing his job, being divorced and being kicked out of his church, it seemed like his entire world was going up in flames. Then one night in a dream, God asked him to pray for his patients. When he awoke in the morning he knew nothing would ever be the same.

Come along on these intriguing adventures as an ordinary paramedic confronts his own skepticism and fear and learns how to hear the voice of God. Get to know Praying Medic, the author, through these stories from his personal spiritual diary. Watch as he learns how to pray for his patients and for strangers in the marketplace.

God's goodness and sense of humor are revealed in these true stories. And you'll witness the transformational power of God as it changes a hardened skeptic into a man of real faith. These stories won't just encourage you—they'll teach you how to live daily in the fullness of God's kingdom.

My Craziest Adventures with God
Volume 2
The Spiritual Journal of a Former Atheist Paramedic

Picking up where Volume One left off, Praying Medic and his wife are back with more stories about their supernatural adventures with God.

Not long ago they were a couple of atheists. Then they met God. After learning about the authority and power believers have been given to heal the sick and work miracles, they began praying with people wherever they went and their lives have never been the same.

Come along on their adventures with Jesus and the Holy Spirit. Discover how an unexpected invitation to travel to Brisbane, Australia, brought them into working on the streets—alongside dedicated local church volunteers—praying for men and women in homeless shelters and on the streets.

Watch as these ordinary believers see the sick healed, the mentally ill set free, and demonic forces beaten. From healing, to automotive miracles, time alteration, and financial miracles, nothing is off limits for God.

You'll be laughing one minute and crying the next as the extravagant love of God is poured into the lives of the people you'll meet in these stories.

A Kingdom View
of Economic Collapse

If you'd like to learn about economic collapse, but you're tired of being lured into investing scams, and hearing warnings about God's judgment, this may be the book you've been looking for.

In his usual no-nonsense style, Praying Medic gives readers a crash course in economics and finance, explaining things in terms the average person can understand. He provides an overview of historic cases of economic collapse and determines which nations are at risk today. He examines the cause of the recent Greek debt crisis and shares the lessons to be learned from it. He shares a number of prophetic dreams about economics and finance, and offers suggestions about how we might rebuild after a collapse, if one were to happen. The final chapter discusses how the kingdom of God ought to respond to crisis.

Topics covered in this book:
- God's purposes for economic crisis.
- Why governments print so much money.
- A prophetic look at our economic future.
- A simple lesson on finance and economics.
- The role of the International Monetary Fund.
- A look at historic cases of economic collapse.
- How central banks and the Federal Reserve operate.
- Which nations are currently at risk for economic collapse.
- How we might rebuild in the aftermath of an economic collapse.
- How the Greek debt crisis happened and lessons to be learned from it.

American Sniper:
Lessons in Spiritual Warfare

Drawing upon scenes from the popular film American Sniper, Praying Medic gives readers a look inside the mind of a well-prepared kingdom soldier.

Relying on the use of analogy and symbolism, the author compares the life of a Navy SEAL to the life of a believer. The book closely follows the script of the film. With each scene the author illustrates principles of spiritual warfare, drawing from his own life experiences and from many spiritual dreams he's had.

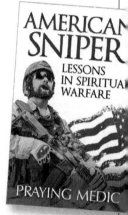

The goal of this book is to help believers assess their state spiritual preparedness and identify any deficiencies they might have. Resources are recommended for further training and equipping, if needed.

Because so many lives have been devastated by the kind of emotional trauma portrayed in the film, the last chapter includes a simple approach to healing emotional trauma that can be used by virtually anyone.

Whether you're in a position of church leadership or just someone who wishes to be better trained and equipped for ministry, this book will add a few more tools to your arsenal.

43784470R00026

Made in the USA
Lexington, KY
02 July 2019